# THE CART
## That Carried Martin

Eve Bunting • Illustrated by Don Tate

ini Charlesbridge

*To my daughter, Christine*
—*E. B.*

*For Grandpa*
—*D. T.*

**Author's Note**
In April 2008 I read an article called "King's Funeral Wagon Carries Interesting Tale," published by the *Atlanta Journal-Constitution*. The words of journalist Jim Auchmutey inspired me to further explore the subject and create what has now become this book. I hope *The Cart That Carried Martin* does justice to the poignant story of Dr. King's funeral.

Text copyright © 2013 by Eve Bunting
Illustrations copyright © 2013 by Don Tate
All rights reserved, including the right of reproduction in whole or in part in any form. Charlesbridge and colophon are registered trademarks of Charlesbridge Publishing, Inc.

Published by Charlesbridge
85 Main Street
Watertown, MA 02472
(617) 926-0329
www.charlesbridge.com

Library of Congress Cataloging-in-Publication Data
Bunting, Eve, 1928–
    The cart that carried Martin/Eve Bunting; illustrated by Don Tate.
        p. cm.
    ISBN 978-1-58089-387-9 (reinforced for library use)
    ISBN 978-1-60734-601-2 (ebook)
1. King, Martin Luther, Jr., 1929–1968—Death and burial—Juvenile literature.  I. Tate, Don, ill.  II. Title.
E185.97.K5B785 2013
323.092—dc23      [B]      2012026688

Printed in China
(hc) 10 9 8 7 6 5 4 3

Illustrations done in pencil and gouache on watercolor paper
Display type set in Truesdell by the Monotype Corporation Ltd.
Text type set in Myriad Pro by Adobe Systems Inc.
Color separations by KHL Chroma Graphics, Singapore
Printed by Imago in China
Production supervision by Brian G. Walker
Designed by Diane M. Earley

## The cart was old.

Its paint had faded.

It was for sale outside Cook's Antiques and Stuff.

Nobody wanted it.

Then two men came along.

"This is exactly what we're looking for," one said.

"We'll buy it."

But the store was closed.

They came by again.

The store was still closed.

"We'll borrow it," the first man said.

"We can't do that," the other replied.

"We can. We'll bring it back when he's finished with it."

A truck was brought to take away the cart.

Friends painted it green.

"It's the color of grass when it rains," a woman said.

"He would like that," said a man.

The cart was moved again and parked at the Ebenezer
Baptist Church.

Waiting.

Two mules were hitched to the cart.

The mules' names were Belle and Ada.

"Ordinary mules for an ordinary funeral," the people told
one another. "That was what he wanted."

"The mule is a symbol of freedom," someone said.
"Each slave was promised a mule and forty acres when he was freed."

Crowds surrounded the church, waiting in the April
morning for the service to begin.
   Many could not get inside.
   They climbed trees,
      and lampposts,
         and stop signs.
   They stood on parked cars.
   The roof of a Cadillac collapsed under some of them.

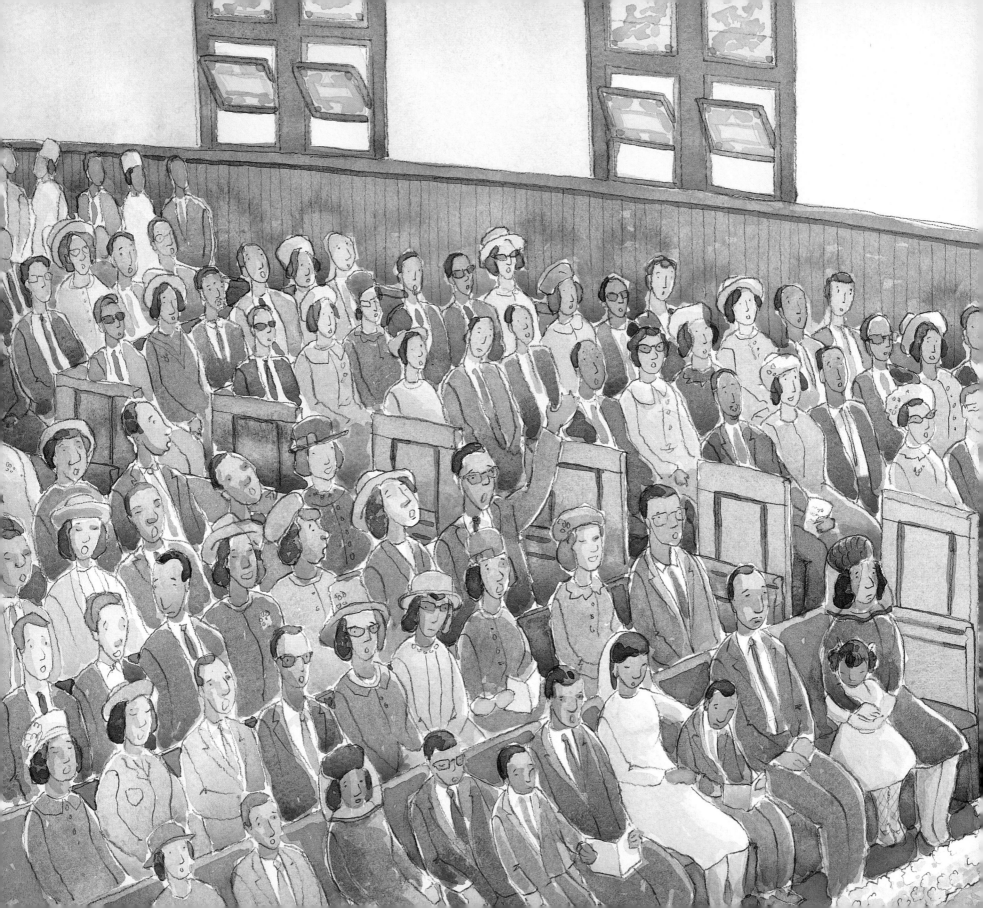

The church throbbed with the sounds of singing.
The songs were not sad, but there was a terrible
sadness in them anyway.
Men and women and children wept.

The mules stood almost motionless.

They flicked only their ears as the coffin was carried from the church and placed in the cart.

At the command, Belle and Ada began pulling.

The cart was not heavy.

The coffin was not heavy.

The man inside it was not heavy.

His great spirit had been the heaviest part of him.

It could not be kept in a coffin.

The cart rolled through the streets of Atlanta, past the Georgia state capitol.

Sometimes the crowds sang as it passed.

"We shall overcome," they promised.

Sometimes they stood in a holy silence, and the only sound was the rumble of wooden wheels.

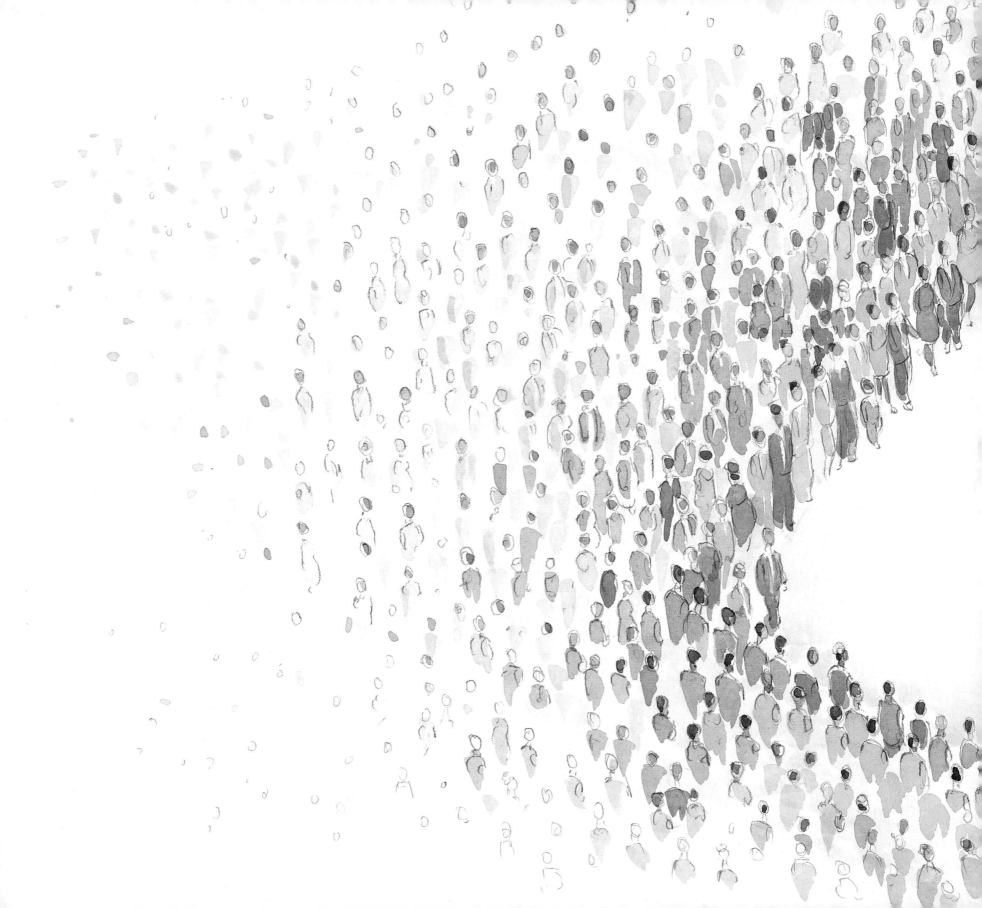

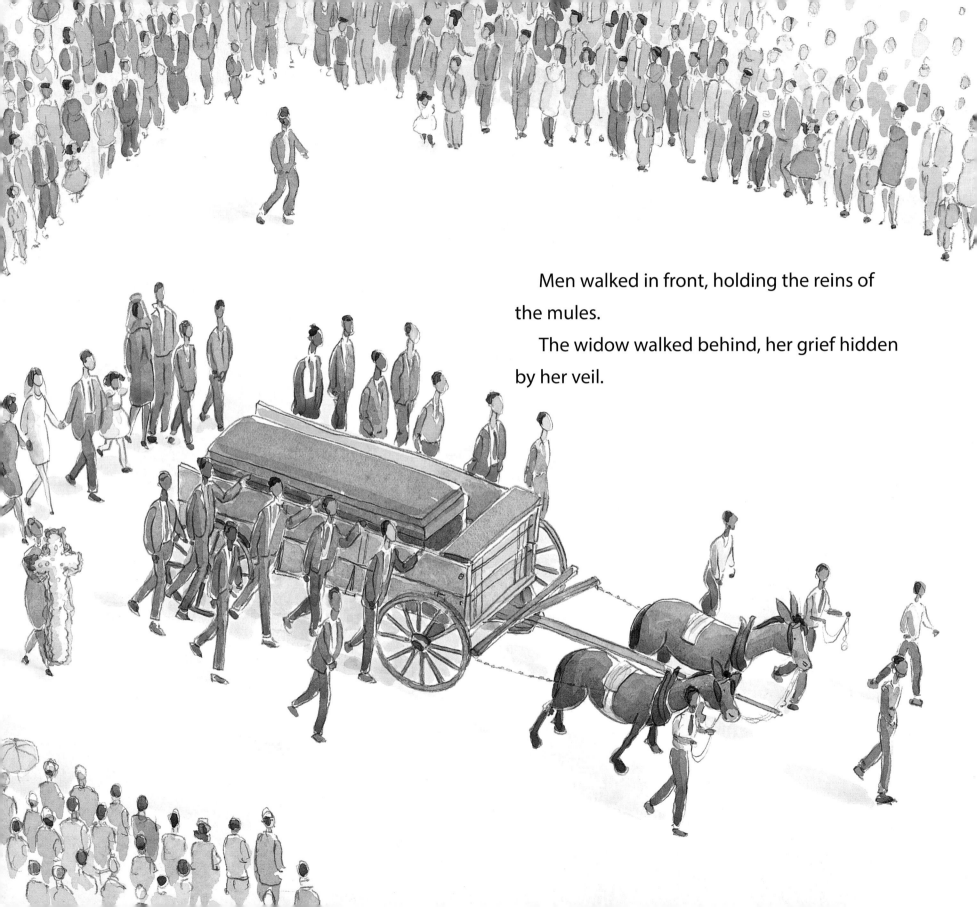

Men walked in front, holding the reins of the mules.

The widow walked behind, her grief hidden by her veil.

At Morehouse College the mules obeyed the command to stop.

The coffin was taken into the college quadrangle for a second service.

Outside the college another crowd pressed forward.

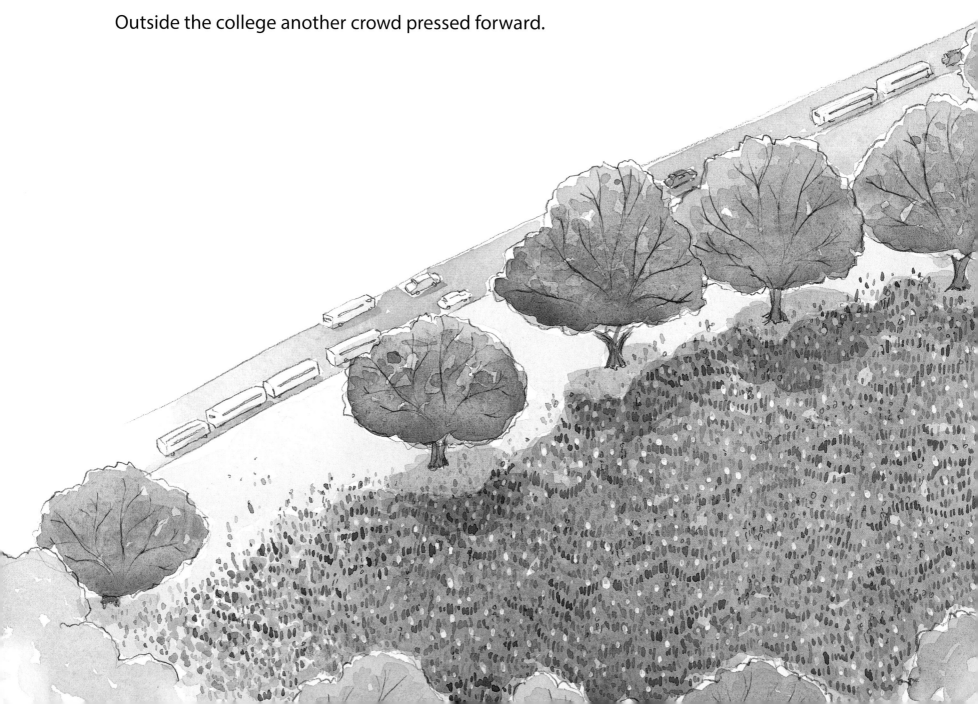

Bells pealed.

More people sang.

The second service ended.

The coffin was carried out and placed in a hearse for the drive to the cemetery.

"Is it over?" someone asked.

"It will never be over," replied another. "What he stands for lives on."

Belle and Ada were taken back to the farm. For them it was over.

The simple wooden cart was returned to Cook's Antiques and Stuff.

It had only been borrowed.

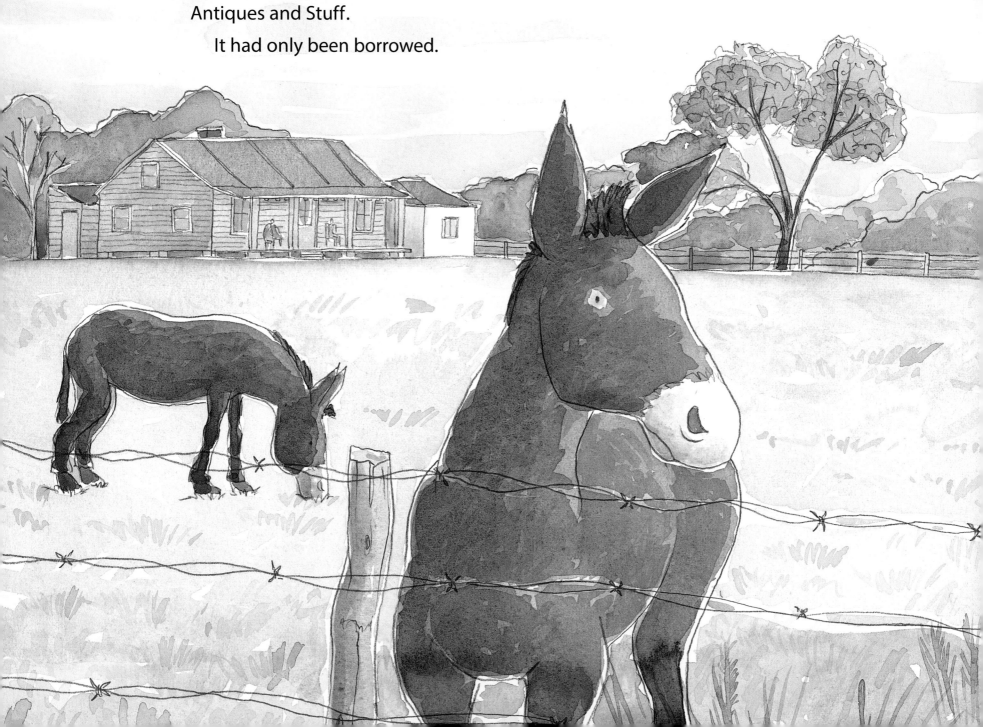

Now there were many offers to buy it.
In the end it was sold to the King family and placed
in the Martin Luther King Jr. National Historic Site.

People walk around the cart now.
They lean across the velvet rope that separates it
from the crowd. They stare. Men take off their caps.

This is the humble cart that, not so long ago,
carried greatness.

## *About Dr. Martin Luther King Jr.*

Dr. Martin Luther King Jr. was born in Atlanta, Georgia, on January 15, 1929. During his short life he fought for racial justice by peaceful means. Among the many honors he received was the Nobel Peace Prize in 1964. He always strove to feed the hungry and to love and serve humanity.

There were, however, those who did not believe in his lifelong dream of racial equality. Dr. King was assassinated on April 4, 1968, shot to death as he stood on a motel balcony in Memphis, Tennessee. President Lyndon B. Johnson declared April 7 a day of national mourning in Dr. King's memory.

Tens of thousands of people marched behind Dr. King's funeral casket on April 9, 1968, as it was carried in a farm cart for three and a half miles through Atlanta. Crowds waited outside the Ebenezer Baptist Church where both Dr. King and his father had been pastors. They waited again outside Morehouse College, where Dr. King had gone to school. He was laid to rest in South-View Cemetery, a burying place founded by former slaves.

Dr. King's wife, Coretta Scott King, continued his work for social justice and devoted her life to his legacy.